I0002664

Applying

SOA Principles in Informatica®

Table of Contents

1

Introduction

Foreword

Agreed, there are many books on Service Oriented Architecture (SOA). Most of these books discuss implementation of SOA either as a vendor-neutral framework or with regard to the programming language such as Java. But the IT world has evolved a lot since Java was first introduced. The evolution of Data Warehousing has brought in a whole new set of technologies to the mix. Extract, Transform and Load (ETL) tools in particular have evolved from purely transformation engines to high performing data integration/processing engines. Software such as Informatica PowerCenter have evolved from pure ETL tools to Data Integration (DI) engines that are capable of processing enterprise data at faster speeds through a robust and reliable framework. Beyond the traditional relational databases and flat files, these data integration engines provide out of the box connectivity to legacy systems (such as mainframes), technology standards (such as LDAP), messaging queues (such as JMS), enterprise applications (such as SAP), cloud based applications (such as Salesforce.com), social media applications (such as Facebook) and Hadoop. Evolution of these DI engines has created a need to revisit the way we have traditionally implemented SOA in the enterprise. SOA can now be delivered faster on a more reliable platform with unlimited scalability – all with the same set of developers and expertise that the organizations already have.

Imagine an organization's need to build a "Legacy Wrapper Service" around a mainframe. A Legacy Wrapper Service is intended to wrap around a legacy system to

eliminate any direct access to it. Elimination of this dependency makes it easy to retire the legacy system and also enables the consumers of the system transparent of the data store for any future upgrades. Eventually, when the system is retired, the legacy wrapper service will be pointed to the new system/data store – effectively having all of its consumers upgraded in one go. The requirements for building such a service at the minimum will be to establish a reliable connectivity to the mainframe, read the data off of it, transform the data format into a relational format (as an example), and expose the data, say, as a web service. Consumers can then be redesigned to use this web service instead of directly accessing the mainframe. Even though the core requirement is only to build a wrapper around the legacy system, there is an implicit requirement to perform the data transformation so as to convert the mainframe COBOL format into an open format like XML. Advantage of such a transformation is that the consumers do not have to worry about the details of the actual data stored in the background and can purely focus on the business logic. Now, for a team of programmers to develop such a solution, they would need to perform at least the following major activities:

- Establish connectivity to mainframes
- Read data off mainframes and parse it using COBOL layout
- Transform the data into XML format
- Expose the program as web service

Now, each of the above steps requires a different skill set and the whole task obviously requires multi-faceted resources. Besides the technical capabilities to perform the above steps, testing itself is a huge challenge because each of the above steps requires a different set of test cases. It is very important to note that the effort spent in designing and developing the code to transform the data into XML format is only a small portion of the overall effort. Additionally, the code needs to be tested for its reliability, scalability and performance, and benchmarks need to be established. Now consider the alternate of using a Data Integration tool such as Informatica PowerCenter to build such a service:

- Establish connectivity to mainframes → an out of the box connectivity available via PowerExchange

- Read data off mainframe and parse it using COBOL layout → an out of the box functionality is usually available to parse the layout from the source and translate to PowerCenter universal data format
- Transform the data into XML format → out of the box transformations such as XML Generator can be used to generate XML content from PowerCenter universal data format
- Expose the program as web service → a Web Service Hub is setup in which any PowerCenter mapping can be exposed as a web service

Assuming that PowerExchange and Web Service Hub are already setup in a given environment, developing such a legacy wrapper service (in its simplest form) is only a matter of minutes compared to the tedious programming approach. Also, consider the time it takes to test both the solutions. With the PowerCenter solution, the only element that will be tested is the true logic behind the transformation to XML, whereas in the programming approach, more time is spent on connectivity and the web service exposure than the pure transformation part of it. This example is not intended to showcase the DI technologies as a replacement for programming languages or as a one-stop solution for all programming needs. This example just highlights the need to revisit the technology usage for Data Integration needs. After all, one of the fundamental drivers for SOA is the need to reduce the time spent on integrating applications.

SOA is a costly and long term investment, from which an organization does not benefit directly. But its value is undeniable. When an organization merges with another, and needs a new system integrating the existing ones, the benefits of SOA can be felt. This book takes a drastic new look at implementation of the SOA in a very cost effective manner by leveraging off the shelf products which provide a great head start in development and reliable means of maintenance.

What does this book cover?

This book does not attempt to solve all the SOA problems by proposing Informatica products as solution, instead it looks at the SOA problems that can be solved with

Informatica products and attempts to explain implementation approaches for the same. This book assumes the reader to be familiar with the Informatica product suite. While the reader is not expected to be very experienced with these products, a basic understanding of what the product does is assumed. Each section of this book addresses one or more SOA principles and design patterns and discusses a possible solution using Informatica product suite. Reader is advised to know that there may be several other alternative solutions that are not discussed in this book. This book does not aim to arrive at the best Informatica product based solution for each SOA principle and design pattern. However, it strives to provide a starting point to Informatica product consumers in solving their SOA problems.

Before you read this book...

This book uses the conventions and design patterns as discussed by Thomas Erl and others in the SOA Design Patterns and other books published by Prentice Hall as its base standard. While it does not try to re-interpret the patterns discussed in those books, it tries to apply Informatica context to the same. Hence some contents referred here may be copyrighted by Prentice Hall.

How is this book organized?

This book begins by setting context for Services in the new age. How we design, develop and maintain a service has drastically changed as the technologies evolved. Hence this book begins by introducing different services in the context of the new technologies. There are several Informatica products that help develop a specific type of service. For example, Informatica's PowerCenter can be used to build enterprise level Data Integration services and Informatica's Data Quality product can be used to build sophisticated Data Quality services. The second chapter of this book discusses various Informatica products and the specialised services that can be built using them. In chapter 3, the book discusses various SOA design principles and how they can be implemented using various Informatica products. Chapter 4 discusses SOA Design Patterns in the context of Informatica products.

Scope of this book

SOA is more than Informatica products. Informatica products offer technology and functionality that is above and beyond SOA. The scope of this book is only limited to the overlap of the Service Oriented Architecture and the features & functionality of Informatica products related to it.

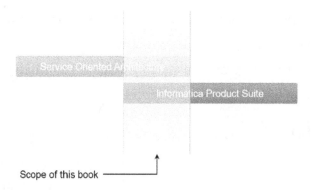

Within the Informatica product suite, this book focuses only on some of the products, that too only SOA related features of the products. This book does not intend to teach you Informatica products. Purchasing this book does not entitle you to any free license of Informatica software

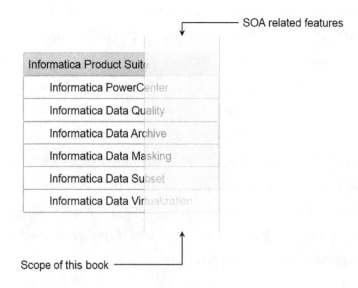

SOA or not?

One of the fundamental principles of SOA is to be vendor neutral, however this book's primary focus is to help build SOA services using Informatica product suite. While this appears as a contradiction, this, in fact, is only a supplement. The book's primary purpose is to help those who would like to build services using any of the Informatica products.

Terminology used

Some terminology used inside this book is very similar to some of the products and/or product features provided by Informatica. Hence it is important to understand what the author is actually referring to. Unless otherwise stated, the term "Mapping Service" refers to a mapping that is used as part of a Workflow that is published as a Service and not to the Informatica feature named *Mapping Service*. Similarly, "Workflow Service" refers to a workflow that is published as a Service and not any Informatica product feature.

Acknowledgements

I owe my first and largest debt to my wife, Divya, who supported my efforts way beyond what was fair to expect. Thank you. Your name belongs on the cover of this book every bit as mine does. I also want to thank Thomas Erl, the author of SOA Design Patterns by Prentice Hall. He is every bit of inspiration for me to write this book

Contacting the author

Author can be reached at author@powercenterbook.com

Linked In: Keshav Vadrevu

Introduction to PowerCenter

PowerCenter is a Data Integration engine that can perform high speed data extraction, transformation and loading. Its rich GUI based Integrated Development Environment allows rapid development with minimal code. PowerCenter has an extensive transformation language and its code does not need to be compiled. Using vibe virtual data machine underneath, PowerCenter allows universal data access. In other words, a mapping can be written to access one data store and can be modified to access another data store without affecting rest of the logic.

PowerCenter architecture is based on client-server model. It consists of PowerCenter server and PowerCenter client tools. Below is a list of all of the components that are part of the PowerCenter architecture

PowerCenter Domain

In its simple terms, Domain can be defined as an environment. You will have a PowerCenter domain for each environment. For example, if you have Development, Test and Production environments, you essentially create 3 different domains – one for each environment. Domain information is stored in a set of tables, which are created and configured as part of PowerCenter server installation. These domain tables store metadata related to services within the PowerCenter, users, groups, etc...

Informatica Node

A node is a machine participating in the Informatica Domain. Typically, a node consists of CPU, Memory and Disk. A node can be active or passive depending on the services it is hosting. Informatica domain can consist of more than one node. These nodes can host a wide variety of operating systems such Windows, Linux, HP-UX, etc. Informatica server software is installed on each node participating in a domain.

PowerCenter Services

A domain consists of several services, such as license service, PowerCenter Repository Service and PowerCenter Integration Service. Each of this service provides a unique functionality to clients.

PowerCenter Repository Service (PCRS)

A PowerCenter Repository is a set of tables created when your Informatica Administrator creates a PowerCenter Repository Service during post installation process. The entire code that a developer builds is stored inside the repository. Repository contains hundreds of tables, whereas PowerCenter stores the developer's code within these tables very intelligently. It is hard to manually look at these tables and comprehend and hence, they should be left alone unless there is a dire need to look at them. Along with developer's code, repository also contains metadata like definitions of the tables used by the mappings, source and target connections, etc...

When the developer runs a Workflow (a job in PowerCenter), its information is fetched from the repository. Thereafter, the runtime statistics are stored back in the repository again. Hence the repository is a key and live element in PowerCenter architecture

PowerCenter Integration Service (PCIS)

An integration service is the engine that actually runs PowerCenter workflows (jobs). Integration services continuously interact with PowerCenter Repository to fetch the information of the job it is about to start and keeps the repository up-to-date regarding the status of the job, including the processed row counts. Each workflow is assigned to an integration service. Each integration service can run one or more workflows at the same time. Workflows can also be scheduled to run on Integration Service at specific date/time.

Grid

A grid is a collection of nodes. A PowerCenter Integration Service can run upon an individual node or on a grid. When an Integration Service runs on a grid, it automatically load balances the workflows that it is executing, such that the resources (nodes) are optimally utilized. When a node in the domain fails, integration service can be configured to failover the workflows running on that node to another node(s) to provide a seamless failover of the jobs.

Putting it all together

Now that we have a basic understanding of each component, let's take a look at it all together. See the picture below.

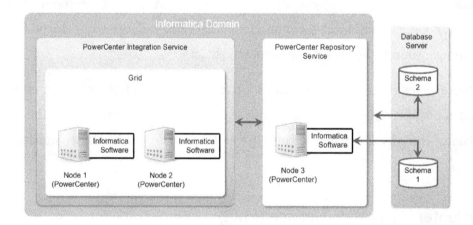

The above picture represents a single Informatica domain, containing 3 nodes. Out of these, two nodes (node 1 and node 2) are participating together to form a grid. An integration service is running atop of this grid. Node 3 is hosting a PowerCenter repository service, whose repository tables lie in the schema 1 of the database server. The schema 2 of the same database server hosts the domain metadata tables. Informatica server software is installed on all the 3 nodes.

While there are many possible configurations for the given nodes, the one above is an example for understanding how the components fit together in the Informatica PowerCenter architecture.

PowerCenter objects

As mentioned before, PowerCenter Repository consists of several tables that hold the different objects created using PowerCenter client tools. In this section of the book, we look at different types of objects that can be created in a PowerCenter repository using various client tools. With a few exceptions, objects in repository are hierarchical in nature as discussed below.

Folders

Folders are the top level objects that can be created within a repository. A folder consists of several objects that form PowerCenter code. Most of the objects created by a developer during the lifecycle of development are stored within a folder. This includes mappings, sessions and workflows. It is typical to have a folder for each project being developed in the repository. It is not uncommon for customers to have hundreds of folders in the same repository, even though the performance of such a repository depends on the amount of objects within each folder and the number of users connected to it at any given time. Examples of folder names are:

→ DataWarehouse
→ DataMart
→ ProjectX
→ CustomerInfoDB

Sources

Sources are table definitions imported from a database into the PowerCenter repository. These table definitions are used while developing mappings to define the attributes to read from. Once imported, the table definitions remain independent of the underlying database. Hence, if a table definition in the source database changes, it needs to be re-imported again. Sources are stored within folders. Thus, a source can be imported into multiple folders. In which case, each definition is unique and must be maintained separately. Sources can be grouped into data sources. They must be unique within a data source. So, within a given data source in a given folder, there can be only one source having a certain name. Developers can organize the sources into different data sources as they see fit. However, each source definition can be associated with only one data source. The same data source can be imported into PowerCenter repository under different data sources. For example, a source table "employees" can exist in data sources "Data Warehouse" and "Data Mart". These two table definitions need not be identical. But "Data Warehouse" data source itself cannot have two tables of the name "employee".

Targets

Conceptually similar to sources, targets are table definitions imported into PowerCenter repository to define what attributes are being written to. Targets are also stored within folders, although they do not have any grouping (such as data sources). Hence, every target definition within a folder must be unique, where uniqueness is defined by the table name.

Transformations

Transformations are not only the most fundamental objects in PowerCenter repository but are also the most important. Fundamentally, a transformation processes the data. This includes modifying data, reordering it, transposing it and, in some cases, generating it as well. There are several built-in transformations such as sorter, rank and aggregator. But developers can also build custom transformations and embed java code into PowerCenter. Each transformation is built to perform one unique operation on data. Developer can combine any permissible combinations of these transformations to meet their data processing needs

Ports

Columns in transformations are known as ports. Data once read from a data source is converted into PowerCenter's universal data format. All the transformations exchange information through the ports. While writing the data to the target, PowerCenter Integration Service converts the data from universal format to native format of the target databases. Therefore, the source and targets contain columns, whereas the transformations contain ports.

Mappings

Mappings are units of code that read data off one or more sources, optionally transform it and write it to one or more targets. A mapping, in its simplest form, is a data flow that defines how the data moves from a given source to a given target and how it is to be transformed in between. In a simple pass through mapping, the data is written as-it-is to the target without any changes. In a more complex mapping, data may perform change detection, then sort, aggregate and finally calculate summary of transactions and load them to the target.

Mapplets

Mapplets are reusable mappings. While a mapping has one or more sources and targets, mapplets have generic inputs and outputs. Hence a mapplet by itself cannot used in a session. A mapplet must be used in a mapping to be able to execute it. While a mapping can be used to created many sessions and hence considered reusable, mapplet allows the flexibility of reusing a set of transformations without defining specific source or targets

Session Task

When a mapping is created, the developer defines the data flow from a source to a target with or without transformations in between. These source and target definitions might have been imported previously using the source analyzer and the target designer. It is important to note that while doing so, PowerCenter only imports the table definition and does not retain the connectivity information such as the database name, user name, password. This is ideal because when a developer imports table definitions, he/she might have done so with their individual logins which usually have read only access to data. However, when the job runs, we would like it to use an application having write access to it. This keeps the application independent of any individual credentials. So the connectivity to the source and the target needs to be specified to be able to execute the mapping. This is exactly where the session fits in. A session contains connectivity and runtime information for a mapping. The session itself does not have any code but it is linked to a mapping and associates the runtime configuration to it. While a mapping defines "how" the data flows, session defines "where" the data comes from and where it goes. A session also defines other runtime metadata such as commit interval, schema/owner name overrides, etc.

Workflows

A workflow defines the logical order of execution of tasks such as sessions. While a session itself is linked to a mapping and hence indirectly defines the data flow between a source and target, most data integration applications are usually more complex than interacting with a single source/target.

When there are multiple sessions involved, there usually is an order in which they need to be executed. For example, before loading transactions data, one has to ensure that the customers' and products' data for the corresponding transactions is up-to-date. This ensures the data integrity and avoids any key violations. Hence, a workflow is created where the order in which the sessions need to be executed can be defined. Sessions can be configured to run in sequence or in parallel or a combination of both.

Worklets

 A worklet is to a workflow what a mapplet is to a mapping. Worklet is a group of session tasks. Worklets can be reused within one or more workflows.

2

Services in the Data Integration Environments

"Services are units of logic independent from each other and implement only one action"

Defining a Service

Defining a service is much easier in theory than in practice. This is probably the most elementary and the most complex question when implementing SOA with non-traditional technologies such as Informatica PowerCenter. Typically, when dealing with SOA, we refer to services as enterprise entities. When using Informatica technology suite, services come in all shapes and sizes. Let's take a look at some of the use-cases below:

- Shared Services team would like to build a service that returns a standardized country name for a given country code

- A business unit wants to build a service that processes an invoice when an invoice number is given
- Compliance team would like to build a service that takes customer information as input and masks any sensitive field and returns masked data back.

In a typical programming world, all these implementations are interfaced with a main class containing a main function. Depending on the complexity of the logic involved, this main class may rely on one or more class/jar files. In a non-programming world, it is much more complicated than that. Now consider the examples above being built using technologies such as Informatica PowerCenter. For the first two requirements, each of this solution will be a workflow. Depending upon the complexity of the logic involved, this workflow may contain one or more mappings within it. However, for the third requirement, an Informatica Product such as Dynamic Data Masking® can be used to provide this service out of the box. Technologies like Informatica PowerCenter® and Dynamic Data Masking® are built to enable developers to rapidly develop solutions that are easy to run and maintain. To provide such capability, these technologies use a very different approach to build solutions. Hence, a new thought process is needed when building services with such technologies. This new thought process also changes how and what we look upon as a service depending on the service we build. In this chapter, we discuss different kinds of services that can be built using various Informatica products. True use cases for these types of services and their implementation approaches are discussed in detail in upcoming chapters.

As we will see in detail later, we will regard workflows in any Informatica product (such as PowerCenter) as a service. While it is technically possible to build a workflow that does not qualify to be a SOA service, such workflows are out of the scope of this book. This book looks at many Informatica products – but all of them through the SOA perspective. While there may be several use-cases for many Informatica products and/or features, only the ones that are useful for SOA implementations are discussed in this book.

This chapter of the book introduces several Informatica products that we discuss later on. Each of these products is used in its own way for successful SOA implementation. Not all products are needed to build a service. But this book attempts to cover the suggested technologies for different kinds of services. For example, a data integration service and a data quality service can both be built using Informatica PowerCenter, however using right technologies for the right needs help in building efficient services in faster and reliable way with a low maintenance cost and greater return on investment.

Data Integration Services

For the services to be truly enterprise-class, they must be built with SOA principles inside out. In this section of the book, we will attempt to understand how different features and components of Informatica architecture can help us build different kinds of services. It is important to note that unless otherwise stated, Data Integration Services in this book refers to any service built in Informatica's Data Integration technologies (like PowerCenter) and not the Informatica's product feature named Data Integration Service (used along with Model Repository to run DQ jobs). Reusability is the core principle for building services. Hence, we begin by taking a look at different levels of reusability available in Informatica PowerCenter. The picture below shows a hierarchy of the objects that can be created in PowerCenter alongside the reusable components of each of the objects.

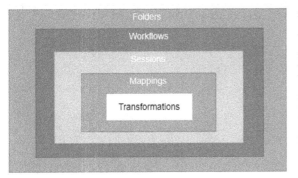 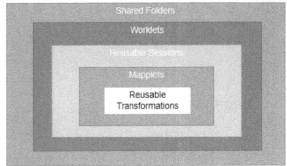

As shown in the above diagram, PowerCenter offers reusability at every level of the product. Typically each workflow can be regarded as a service (web service or otherwise). Now each of this service can be comprised of one or more components (Worklets, tasks, mappings, etc...). So, the simplest service will be one workflow containing one session (and hence one mapping). This mapping may or may not contain reusable transformations within it. However, while building a workflow, each mapping in itself should be looked upon as a service and SOA principles must be applied on it to the meaningful extent. So, every mapping service (not to be confused with the Informatica's mapping service feature) will have its own contracts (inputs and outputs) with its action well defined. Let's use the picture below as an aid to understand this:

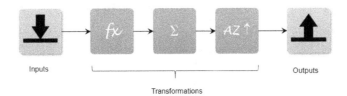

A mapping service, has atleast one or more input interfaces (sources), one or more output interfaces (targets) and necessary transformations in between. It is possible that the input and output interface of a mapping is one and the same as the workflow service it belongs to. This happens when the service (workflow) contains only one session. Though, often more than one mapping may be required to build a service in PowerCenter, in which case, the service may look a little more complex than above.

Data Quality Services

Conceptually the same, data quality services are usually built in the Informatica Developer tool (next generation platform) on same lines as a PowerCenter mapping. However, services developed in Developer tool can exist as standalone services within developer or can be embedded as components into PowerCenter mappings, thus allowing them to be part of PowerCenter Services. Data Quality Services can leverage several out of the box features to parse, match and standardize the data.

Data Archive Services

Typically, Data Archive jobs are stand-alone jobs that run at different intervals than usual data integration or data quality services. The need for a data archive job to be exposed as a service usually occurs when there is a need to perform live archive in the midst of a processing. For such cases, data archive jobs can be exposed as components, both into PowerCenter mappings and workflows. HTTP transformation can be used to invoke the data archive components from within a mapping. When an archive component needs to be executed between PowerCenter mappings but still part of the same workflow service, it can be executed via a command task.

Masking and Subset Services

Informatica's Persistent Data Masking can receive sensitive data (such as credit card numbers) and mask them so that the original sensitive data is protected. Informatica's Data Subset services are used for Test Data Management to extract subsets of data from a master dataset. This is extremely helpful to bring data from production environments to non-production environments without losing the data integrity. Masking and Subset tasks rely on the PowerCenter framework to execute the masking and subset functionality respectively. Hence, Masking and Subset services are typically PowerCenter services executing as PowerCenter workflows. Masking functionality can also be exposed as components (transformations) within existing PowerCenter services.

Virtual Data Services

Virtual data services help expose existing data stores and data integration logic as services that can be consumed by other SOA services. They can be built using the Informatica Data Services™ framework in next generation platform

3

Service Oriented Design Principles

Standardized Service Contracts

"Service contract is an agreement between a service and its consumers for a successful information exchange"

Irrespective of the technology that is used to implement SOA, Standardized Service Contracts play a vital role in a successful implementation. Designing a service contract is one of the first tasks to be performed before actually implementing a service. A contract is to a service what data model is to an ETL application. Contract is a crucial design element that determines how the service will be consumed and also, to a certain extent, defines/restricts its levels of reusability and scalability. Contracts can be defined as sources/targets in PowerCenter and as logical or physical data objects in the Informatica Developer. These objects can be created as reusable objects within shared folders to enable them to be reused within the Informatica domain. Enforcement of the source/target definition is implicit in Informatica products and no additional coding is required. For example, if the source is an XML file, an XSD can be used to import the definition of the XML file. Once imported, no logic needs to be written to parse the input file to read/process XML tags and values. By default, the contracts (source/target) are not tightly coupled with a mapping. It means that the same contract can be reused in several mappings without any additional coding. This also presents a challenge of the contracts being overused causing a negative coupling (unwanted dependency) between the contract (table definitions) and the service logic (mappings). One of the best practices is to separate any service contracts into a folder by themselves (a shared folder) and govern its usage. Strict enforcements are recommended to allow a careful usage of these contracts.

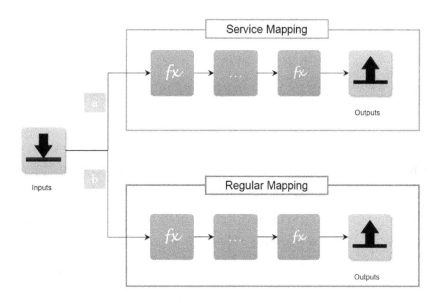

Look at the example above. A single source definition is used in two mappings: one is published as a service, other is not. Reusing table definitions between services and non-services is highly discouraged as this causes a negative coupling between the two mappings. If the regular mapping in this case needs to change, it has a direct impact on the service due to the common source. Similarly, when the service needs to be updated, it has a direct impact on a mapping that is in no way related to it. In the picture above, (b) is the dependency that should be avoided. This dependency can be resolved by creating a different copy of the same input definition – one copy to be used by services and another that can be reused among regular mappings. So, a possible solution for the above will look like this:

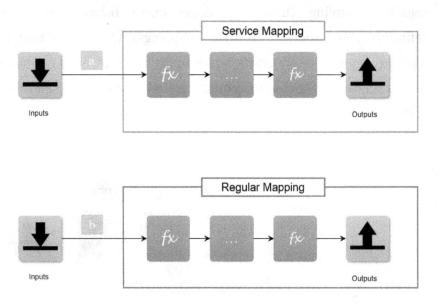

The contract (table definition) that is used by the service mapping can be reused among other services, but not by the mappings that are not published as services. Similarly, the table definition that is used by the regular mapping is not to be used by any service mapping. This will mean that there will be 2 physical copies of the same definition, but the cost of maintenance for these two objects is well justified in the long run by eliminating the dependencies. In an ideal scenario, such dependencies should be avoided one level up by organizing the service and service related objects into a different folder than the regular ones. See the picture below:

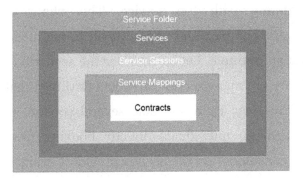 

As shown in the above picture, services should be organized along with their dependencies into a different folder in the repository than the regular objects. However, objects in the corresponding folders should be reused up to a meaningful context.

Service Loose Coupling

"Service loose coupling refers to the ability of the service to reduce the dependency among the service contract, consumers and the service itself"

By default, services are tightly coupled to their contracts/definitions in both Informatica platform. This is primarily due to the metadata driven approach that is used during the design and development in these platforms. When a service changes, its' consumers must be updated to ensure continuity of the information exchange. Similarly, when a service contract is updated (to accommodate new or updated metadata), the service and its consumers must be updated. There are also times when a consumer is more advanced than the service itself and is maintaining a backward compatibility with the service. This chain of dependencies makes the services overly complex and very difficult to maintain. Now, let's look at this scenario with an example. Let us consider the scenario of booking air travel tickets online. There are many service providers (airlines) that provide flight and reservation information. There are also several consumers (travel booking websites, travel agencies, individuals directly booking from airline websites, etc.). Some of these consumers are themselves providers again.

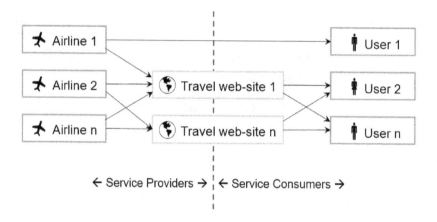

In the above example, each airline is acting as a service provider, whose services are consumed by travel websites (such as Expedia, Kayak...) and also by individuals directly accessing the airline website to make reservations. Travel website 1, in this case, is consuming services provided by all the airlines and is in turn providing services to user 2 and user n. In a complex environment like this, the impact of a change to service contract could break the communication between the service and its consumers and hence potentially impact the business. Now, if Airline 1 has updates to its service contract, it needs to be backward compatible so that travel websites 1 and n do not get affected. Similarly, travel website 1 should also be loosely coupled to its contract so that if the changes are applied to the contract on the travel website side, the underlying logic still remains unaffected and does not impact its communication with other airlines. In real-life scenarios as this, Service Loose Coupling plays a vital role in keeping the communication between the services alive and still allowing the services to expand/upgrade their contracts.

When a service is developed, it needs to use its contract to perform business rules and process the incoming data. So there will always be an intrinsic dependency between the service and the contract. However, this should not stop either service or the contract from evolving independently. When a service and its contract allow each other to evolve independently, the coupling is referred to as positive coupling. Otherwise, it is referred as negative coupling. Based on how a service is built, there are different kinds of coupling – some positive and some negative.

Logic-to-contract (contract-first)

This is a positive coupling because in this type of coupling a service is always built on the contract. In this type of contract, a service contract is first completely defined and a service is built based on the specifications already finalized. The Informatica platform encourages usage of this coupling, since a mapping is considered invalid until the source and target definitions are defined for it.

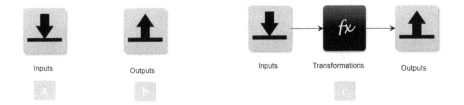

Hence, the contract needs to be in place before the mapping is built. However it is a common practice (often due to time constraints of the project) that development of a service is started with a draft contract and as the contract evolves, so does the service. This practice is highly discouraged due to the fact that the time that is saved at the beginning (and more) is spent later doing modifications and testing a service that is built on half ready contracts. This throws the reliability of the service in to question and also eventually leaves less time for the service to be tested before it goes live.

Contract-to-logic

This type of negative coupling exists when the definition is built on existing logic. While the recommendation is always to build the contract first, at times, a contract is built on a logic that is already exists. This often happens when an existing legacy system such as a mainframe process needs to be published as a service.

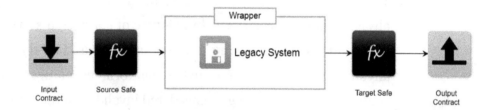

Look at the picture above. A wrapper is built around a legacy system to publish it as a service. Typically in scenarios like this, the goal is to eventually replace the legacy system with minimal or no affect to its consumers. In such a scenario, the wrapper service must be built to be compatible with the legacy system. In the process, the wrapper might carry forward some limitations that originated in the legacy system. This has a direct effect on the service contract as the contract is built around the wrapper logic. Eventually when the legacy system is replaced, the wrapper and the contract must be updated to eliminate the previously known issues and limitations. The primary purpose of the wrapper service is to minimize such a need for change. Hence when contract-to-logic must be applied, adequate precautions need to be taken about the service contract so that the contract is scalable enough even after the legacy system is decommissioned.

Contract-to-implementation

This negative coupling is typically applied when a service contract is designed around an existing data store object such as table(s) or file(s). This is usually the case when the data store object is already used by several processes in the organization and the impact of modifying the existing data store object is significant. This is a common scenario when services are built on existing data warehouses or data marts.

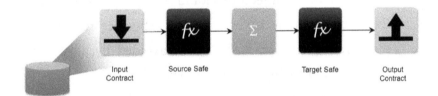

Contract-to-implementation couplings are typically considered negative coupling as the contract is influenced by a data store which creates a certain dependency between the two. However, this is also a common approach taken to publish services out of existing systems, where the service is merely exposing certain data attributes of the data store as part of its contract. Hence eliminating the need for several processes to perform reads and writes from /to the data store. Since the service is purely an interface of the data store, this coupling can be considered positive in the sense that it is creating an abstraction layer on top of the data store.

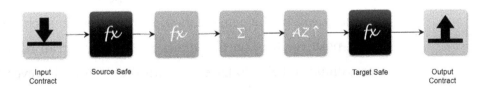

When contract-to-implementation coupling is applied using Informatica PowerCenter or Informatica Developer, it is recommended to have anchor transformations (Source Safe and Target Safe) as they reduce the dependency between the data store and the mapping logic as shown above.

Contract-to-technology

Exposing technology/vendor proprietary information in a contract/definition is a negative form of coupling known as contract-to-technology. Service Oriented Architecture is a vendor-neutral architecture and hence the architecture should be maintained in a vendor-neutral way. Exposing vendor or technology specific parameters is not only discouraged, in fact, it should be avoided by all means. If a service is implemented using a technology like Informatica PowerCenter, an example of such negative coupling is to have lookup cache file names or aggregator cache size, etc. in the input or output contracts.

Contract-to-functional

In an ideal SOA world, consumers merely adapt to the service design and do not influence it. However, there may be cases, where one or more consumers drive the design and development of a service. In such a case, the service is known to have a contract-to-functional coupling. This is common when a service is being built on top of an existing data store such as a Data Warehouse or Data Mart. In such scenarios, typically the service contract and logic is driven by the expectations of the groups that eventually will be the consumers of the services. In such cases, this may have a positive effect on the service as the service can be designed to be more robust and also to have high utilization rate. However, for a service to be enterprise-ready, this kind of coupling should be avoided as much as possible.

Consumer-to-implementation

Typically, consumers of a service access the elements of a service before a service is actually built. It could create a coupling called Consumer-to-implementation. This is considered as negative coupling because of the dependencies between Service objects and non-service objects. In a PowerCenter environment or in the Informatica Developer, this could potentially mean that when a service is built, it is attempting to reuse existing reusable objects.

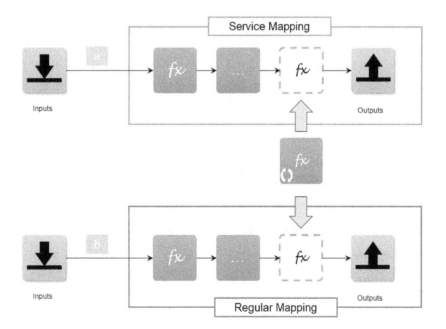

While reusability is good in general sense, in this case, it creates unwanted dependency between a service mapping and a regular mapping. In the example shown above, there are two mappings – a service mapping and a regular (non-service) mapping that have instances of the same reusable transformation. This is a perfect example of consumer-to-implementation, assuming that the regular mapping existed even before service mapping is built. Hence, the service is built with a negative coupling known as consumer-to-implementation. To resolve this dependency, it is recommended to make a copy of the reusable object and use the new copy within the service. This copy can be reused in several services that are eventually built.

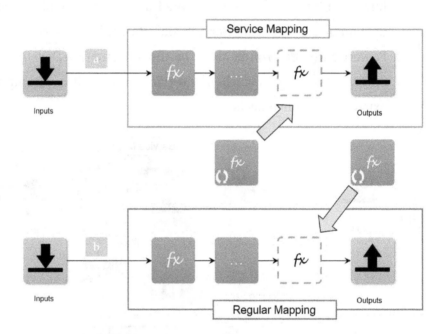

The picture above shows a possible resolution for a consumer-to-implementation coupling. As seen above, a new copy of the reusable transformation is created and one copy is reused among all service mappings whereas another copy is reused across all regular mappings. It is important not to create dependencies between service objects and non-service objects.

Some general guidelines

In Informatica PowerCenter and Developer, one can follow the below guidelines to reduce/eliminate negative coupling:

- Use only necessary ports (columns) from the source in the mappings
- Deliver output for only the ports that are used/modified within the service
- Where applicable, avoid customization of entire SQL queries and try to leverage 'filter' and 'order by' attributes that are defined separately. This will cause the Informatica platform to dynamically generate queries at run time, reducing the dependency on unwanted columns
- Do not bring unwanted columns into lookups and joiners
- Do not carry forward the ports that are no longer needed. If a column is only needed in the first few transformations, do not pass it through all the way to the end

Service Abstraction

"Service abstraction refers to the ability of hiding the underlying service details from the consumers so that loose coupling is preserved"

Abstraction happens in Informatica products at many levels. Services exposed in Informatica platform can be accessed by non-Informatica applications without having to know any of the technical details of the service, except its interface. So, it is safe to say that the services built in Informatica products are by default abstracted. Since Informatica services are built on a reusable framework, it is also important to apply service abstraction to every layer within the service workflow. The simplest way of applying abstraction and reusability within Informatica platform is to build several reusable components and embed these into their parent objects. For example, when abstraction is applied to a PowerCenter mapping, the transformations within the mapping are now moved to a Mapplet and the Mapplet is used within the mapping instead of individual transformations.

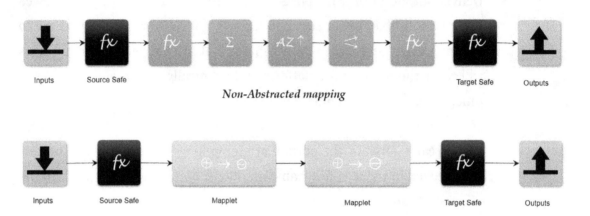

Non-Abstracted mapping

Abstracted mapping

As shown in the picture above, the mapping logic is abstracted into one or more Mapplets. The number of Mapplets is determined by the business logic and the amount of reusability expected out of these Mapplet components. Similar concept can be applied to workflows as well.

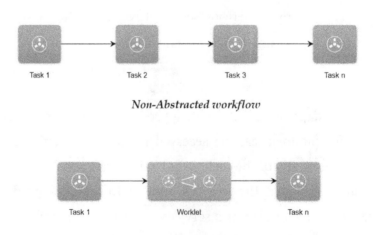

Non-Abstracted workflow

Abstracted workflow

In the example above, a workflow is abstracted by moving the tasks into a Worklet. The advantage of such abstraction is clearly seen with complex mappings/workflows. Abstraction not only makes the objects easier to access without knowing the implementation details, but also helps in increasing the readability of the mappings and workflows, by grouping the objects within them based on the business logic they represent. This also creates a layer of reusability by business logic, so that in future if another service requires the same set of activities to be performed, it can simply reuse the Mapplet/Worklet. These Mapplets/Worklets can also be built in shared folders to create an additional layer of abstraction.

Service Reusability

"Reusability is the ability of the service to participate in several solutions solving different business problems while still staying true to the action it is intended to perform"

There are two aspects of reusability, viz., Reusability within the service and the Service Reusability. Reusability within the service refers to the reusability of the components that comprise the service; while the Service reusability refers to the ability to reuse the service as a whole. Reusability of a service is primarily a design consideration ensuring that the contracts are as generalized as the logic within the service. There are no technical limitations on how services built in Informatica platform can be reused. However, whether or not a service is reused in an enterprise, is primarily driven by several technical and business factors. Technical factors include the ease of using the service without having to develop wrappers or customize the existing service. Business factors include the business problem that the service is built to solve and how frequently this problem is encountered within the enterprise.

Reusable services

Once built, a workflow service, can be leveraged to solve several similar business needs. Informatica platform provide several features that enable such workflow reusability. The most important feature is "Workflow Concurrency". Workflow Concurrency refers to the ability of executing several instances of the same workflow at the same time. At the outset, this does not seem much, but when combined and used with features such as Parameter files, this evolves to be a powerful aspect. With proper design considerations taken into account, a workflow can be built to be dynamic enough to receive several parameters from a parameter file instead of directly being specified within the tasks themselves. So, when such a workflow is enabled for concurrent execution, a different parameter file is passed to each instance, thereby regulating where the workflows sources from or targets to. These parameter files can also be used to regulate and control other aspects of the workflow, such as lookup queries.

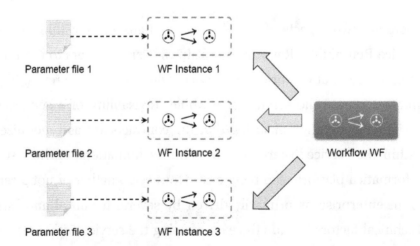

The above picture depicts a workflow published as 3 different instances – each instance running with a different parameter file. This parameter file typically contains different input/output connections, paths (if source/targets are files), lookup connection, and dynamic parameter values and so on. This enables the same service to be published as multiple instances, all using the core logic underneath. Workflow variables along with assignment and decision tasks can also be used to build a dynamic workflow service. For better control, each of these instances can be named so that that particular instance can be tracked, monitored and audited for future purposes.

Reusability within a Service

A service can only be as reusable as all of the components that it is made up of. Informatica platform have heavily reusable frameworks. This section of the book talks about different capabilities available in Informatica platforms that enable us to build service with highly reusable components. This is not the same as Service Reusability because Service Reusability refers to how we can reuse a service itself to help solve several business problems. The current topic, reusability within a service, however, deals with the components that the service is made up of and focuses on reusing these components across different services. By reusing components across different services, services can be built over a robust set of components.

A service is typically built using several components. A workflow service is built using sessions (mappings) and other tasks (such as command tasks, decision tasks, etc.). Mappings themselves are built using sources, targets and transformations. In both Informatica platform, objects at almost every level can be made reusable.

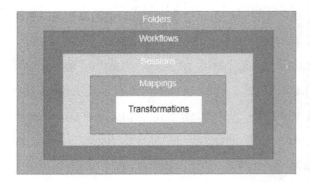 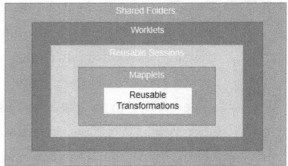

As shown in the picture above, every level of object that can be created has an equivalent object type that is of reusable nature. For example, transformations can be reusable or non-reusable. Reusable transformations are created outside of a mapping and an instance of such transformation is invoked from within a mapping. Non-reusable transformations can be created within a mapping and are limited to the scope of a mapping. A non-reusable transformation created within a mapping can always be promoted as a reusable transformation. Similarly, transformations can be grouped together into Mapplets that can be reused in several mappings. Sessions can also be reusable and used in several workflows or non-reusable and used in a single workflow. Sessions or other tasks can be grouped into Worklets that can be reused across different workflows. Thus every object type within the Informatica platform has corresponding reusable object type.

For a service to be robust, reusable and enterprise class, a clear distinction must be made between the reusable and non-reusable components.

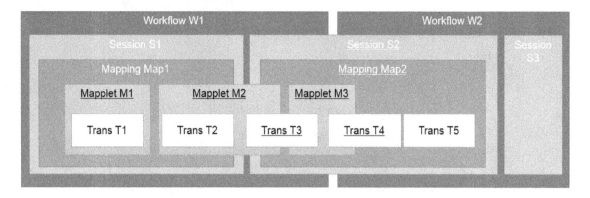

The above picture depicts several layers of reusable (identified with underlined text) and non-reusable objects. Note that for simplicity, Worklets are not represented in this diagram. In the above example, Transformations T1, T2 and T5 are non-reusable, whereas transformations T3 and T4 are reusable. T4 transformation is also reused twice in the same mapping Map2: once as part of mapplet M3 and once directly in the mapping itself. Transformation T5 is non-reusable and is used only in the mapping Map2. Transformation T3 is reused between Mapplets M2 and M3. Mapplets are, by design, reusable components. However, in the above example, Mapplet M1 and M3 are used only once in Mapping Map1 and Map2 respectively, whereas Mapplet M2 is reused by both the mappings Map1 and Map2. At the workflow (service) level, Session S1 is a non-reusable session that is only used once in the workflow W1, whereas Session S2 is a reusable session that is used in both W1 and W2 workflows. W2 also contains a non-reusable session S3. This explains the various levels of reusability available and how a complex mixture of reusable and non-reusable objects can be used within the Informatica platform.

Service Autonomy

> "A Service is autonomous if it has little or no dependency on the resources that it has little or no control on"

To be autonomous, a service must rely as less as possible on external resources that it has no control on. Typically, these resources are databases, flat files or data stores of some kind. Such dependencies cause reliability issues with the service. As the service becomes more and more reusable, it becomes imperative that the service remains autonomous. When resources are shared between the processes and one of the processes continues to perform heavy usage of the shared resource, contention occurs. This contention causes the other process to slow down – most of the times, waiting for the first process to finish its activity. If the shared resource is a data store, one of the following approaches is applied to preserve the service autonomy:

Replicate locally

Cache locally

By replicating locally, we make a copy of the data store that a service is sharing and store it local to the service itself. This causes the service to have full control and unique usage of the service. Another approach is to cache the data store locally and perform periodic refreshes with the main data store. These are two different use-cases used in two different scenarios. When the local data store needs to be in sync with the main data store, it is a good idea to create a replicated copy locally and then perform a database level replication (or another form of lower level replication) between the main dataset and the replicated copy. However, if the service is relying on the data store for read-only purposes, it can simply be cached for faster performance and the cache can be refreshed at regular intervals carefully chosen not to impact the service availability or the service performance.

Replication

The simplest solution for resolving dependency on an external data store is to replicate it locally to the service. As part of this approach, all the data residing in this data store is copied locally. Every time the data store is changed, the changes are replicated in the local copy as well. The latency allowed between these databases depends on the business data stored in and the importance of having that data visible in replicated database as soon as possible. There are several ways to implement such a replication:

Database level replication

If the data store is a relational database, database level replication can be used to sync the changes happening in master database into the replicated database.

Informatica PowerExchange® CDC

Informatica's PowerExchange Change Data Capture product can be used to capture the changes in the source and a PowerCenter mapping can be used to publish these changes in Real-Time to the replicated database.

Informatica Data Replication® (IDR)

IDR is a real-time replication system that is independent of the database platform and is a highly scalable solution. If the data store is an Oracle database, Informatica's Fast Clone® can also be used to read huge volumes of data to be loaded into the replicated database.

Informatica Ultra Messaging® (UM)

Informatica Ultra messaging is an event-based low-latency system that promises zero second latency to transfer events/data between two systems. While Informatica Data Replication® is used to replicate data stores physically, Ultra Messaging® can be used to transfer or sync events between two systems.

Cache

At times, though technically possible, replicating data may not be feasible. Some such scenarios are:

- Sensitive data in the shared database; Replication means increased risk and maintenance
- High performance is required and I/O from the replicated database is not providing enough read throughput

In such scenarios, Informatica platform provide an ability to cache the data so that the replicated data remains in memory for the entire execution of the service. This cache can be made persistent for faster subsequent loads of the service or even for parallel instances of the service running at the same time. These cache files can be "named" so that cache(s) used and maintained by a given service remains unique. Dynamic caches can be built so that the cache files are kept in sync with the changes happening in the primary data store. Dynamic cache allows records in the cache to be dynamically updated at run time to keep up with the primary data store. These caches can be leveraged via a lookup transformation in the mappings so that input data can be looked up against the cache to fetch any additional information. Few caveats that need to be taken into consideration while using cache approach are:

- Caches can go out of sync with the primary data store unless carefully designed

- Caches are good for small to medium sized data sets, but for larger data sets, caches may result in swapping; thus counter effecting the performance
- Caches cannot be queried outside of Informatica platforms, where as a replicated database can be queried separately

Service Composability

"Service Composability principle, when applied, reusable services themselves are composed of other reusable services"

A service composition typically consists of a controller and several contributors. These contributors are built to provide functionality to the controller services and can also act as controllers themselves in other compositions. For the services to be able to act as both, controllers and members, their service contract and the service logic have to be very carefully designed with great emphasis on reusability and scalability. Service Composability differentiates itself from the Service Reusability by focusing on the service's ability to be reused in different compositions with ideally no changes to itself. While being used as part of the composition, the service itself can be either a controller or a contributor. The reusability principle focuses on the ability of the service to be reused with no distinction of being a contributor or a controller.

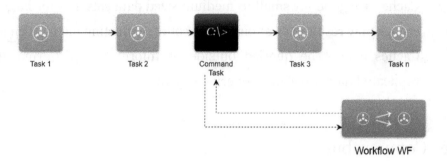

The above picture shows a workflow containing several tasks invoking another workflow using a command task. The command task, in this case, can execute either a workflow service or any other external service via a command line interface. Informatica Informatica platform provide command line interfaces to invoke the workflows. The command task can be synchronous or asynchronous. In synchronous mode, command task will wait for the workflow WF to complete its execution and return back. In an asynchronous mode (no-wait), the command task will invoke the workflow WF and will NOT wait for it to complete. The Workflow WF itself can have another command task that invokes another workflow or external service and so on. This showcases the ability of workflows developed in Informatica PowerCenter to either call or be called by another service.

4

SOA Design Patterns

Design patterns are important in any solution developed using Informatica products –
SOA or not. However, they have a higher significance and emphasis in SOA based
solutions. SOA solutions are built to be reusable enterprise-wide and hence there is a
natural emphasis on reusability which starts with proper design. There are many design
patterns that need to be taken into consideration for a successful SOA implementation.
This book discusses some of them in context of Informatica product suite. While some of
the design patterns are discussed here in a non-traditional way, the focus remains on
enabling the users of Informatica Suite to implement successful SOA solutions.

Agnostic Services

"Agnostic services implement logic that is needed by more than one solution and are usually part of addressing more than one business problem"

Agnostic services implement logic that is needed by more than one solution and are usually part of addressing more than one business problem. Hence separating the agnostic logic from non-agnostic logic plays a key role in determining if and how the service will be reused, at least in part. The distinction must be made very clearly to avoid any misconceptions in the future.

Informatica products such as PowerCenter have built-in features that help designers with this problem. The reusable and non-reusable objects are developed, grouped and maintained separately, making a very clear separation of the intent of the object's original design. For example, transformations that are reusable are designed in the transformation developer, whereas non reusable transformations are directly placed in the mapping itself. Similarly, when more than one transformation is used to build agnostic logic, Mapplets can be used to group them together with a predefined input/output contract (structure). These reusable transformations / Mapplets can further be reused in several mappings in conjunction with logic that is separate (non-agnostic) for each mapping itself.

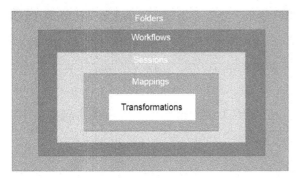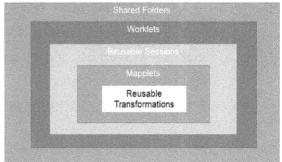

As shown in the picture above, every layer of objects in PowerCenter has an equivalent layer of reusable objects – all the way from folders to transformations. Depending upon the logic that needs to be exposed as reusable components, they can be defined as reusable transformations or Mapplets or reusable sessions or Worklets of shared folders.

Defining a set of reusable components that a service needs to build or needs to reuse ahead of the service development, helps in building robust services on reusable framework. It also helps in defining these reusable objects with a sense of scalability.

In an agile development environment, the clarity of agnostic and non-agnostic logics may develop over a period of time, in which case any non-agnostic objects such as transformations can be converted into reusable objects. When a non-reusable object is converted to reusable object, the parent objects that use them (mappings in this case), will be automatically updated to use an instance of this new reusable object. This "build now reuse later" framework helps develop services in all kinds of lifecycle models.

Often, the business logic to be exposed as an agnostic service is too complex to fit into a single mapping. In such scenarios, the sessions (mappings) can be grouped together into Worklets and reused in more than one workflow/service. When a workflow service consists of logic that is agnostic and non-agnostic, agnostic logic can be placed within a Worklet to differentiate from the non-agnostic logic.

Agnostic Service Declaration

It is not unusual for the design / development cycles of SOA solutions to span across longer periods of time. It is very important to assume that the people involved at the beginning stages of SOA implementation may or may not be involved towards the finishing stages of it. There could be various valid reasons. For example, highly specialized team is needed in the beginning stages to setup a scalable and highly performing solution. But a different or less specialized team may do the job to develop the solution based on the specifications already provided. People also move from one team/place to another, raising a need for new team members to continue the work. Hence it is very important to declare the agnostic and non-agnostic objects and services clearly. PowerCenter allows its users to design, develop, maintain and organize the agnostic and non-agnostic objects with clear distinction. Reusable objects are catalogued differently at every level. See the picture below:

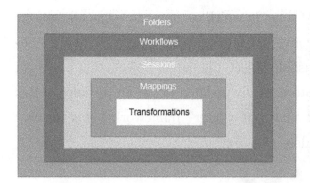 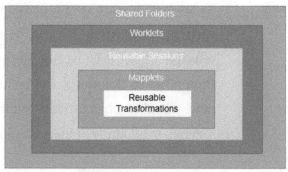

Visual representations are also used to differentiate between reusable and non-reusable objects. A usual practice is also to have shared folders dedicated to contain only reusable objects that can be leveraged in one or more non-shared folders in the repository via shortcuts. Metadata properties can be used to document additional properties of the objects to indicate to future team members on the intent and the suggested usage of the corresponding component. Additionally, naming conventions such as prefixing the objects with "r_" for reusable objects also help to catalogue the reusable objects, thus aiding in easy search and reuse in future.

Atomic Service Transaction

"Service should have the ability to control its transactions without impacting other service calls"

Services should be able to control the transactions they process and determine at run time whether to commit or rollback the data they processed. PowerCenter provides transaction control transformation that allows the services to determine at runtime what to do with the data they have received. Services can choose to commit, rollback or continue the transactions based on logic built into the service itself. This transaction management can also be controlled by setting up a record count based transaction control at the session level that can once again be either dependent on the source data or the data that is generated by the service itself. Now consider an example. Assume that a service is being called to process invoice data. Ideally the service should commit data pertaining to each invoice as and when it has completed its processing. Logic like that can be implemented within a mapping by comparing the current invoice number with previous invoice number and issuing a commit after the last record for the current invoice and before the beginning of the data for next invoice. Complex logic can be built in to the transaction control by using the data being provided by the other transformations in the same mapping or parameters and variables.

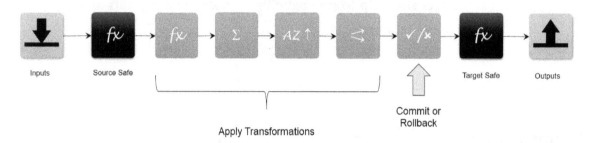

As shown in the picture above, the service can apply several transformation rules and decide, based on the business logic and the resultant data, whether or not to commit it. This gives great control to the service logic to decide on demand the action it needs to perform on the transaction.

When data that is part of the same transaction needs to be transferred between services, either real-time exchange can be made or the data can be stored in a temporary storage that is later read by the subsequent information. For example, if a mapping is invoking another service via a web-service, using a web-service consumer transformation, it can pass the data to the service and receive its response back in real time and determine whether or not to commit the data that it has processed so far. However, if the services are built to execute in a batch mode, data may have to be temporarily written to a file or table, so that the subsequent mapping can read, process this data and write back a response, which is again read by this service. Control data is written along with business data to enable a seamless handshake.

Consider the following use-case to understand such a batch based process hand shake.

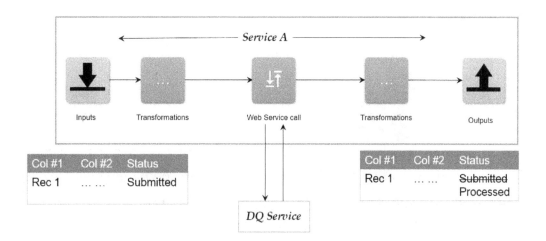

Imagine a Data Quality service "DQ Service" that is invoked by several other services. Now a Service "Service A" needs to pass some customer records to the DQ Service and receive a response back. Only records that are standardized by the DQ Service are loaded to final target and other records are purged out. Such a hand shake can be implemented by building a process control table that is used by both the services. Each service relies on this table for a specific status. For example, Service A will publish records into this table with the status `Submitted`. DQ Service will then lookup on this table for any `Submitted` records and once processed, will change its status to either `Processed` or `Rejected`. Service A will then continue with the records that are of status `Processed` and then respond accordingly.

Service Façade

> "A Service façade is an interface between the service contract and the service itself"

A service façade acts as an interface layer between the service contract and the service itself. This enables the service to be loosely coupled with its contract and thus to be eventually invoked with multiple contracts reusing the same core logic. In a given mapping this can be implemented by pushing the entire logic of the mapping into a Mapplet and using the mapping only to bind the Mapplet with its contract (source / target definitions).

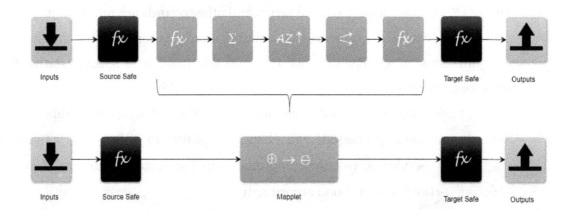

Let's look at the example demonstrated in the picture above. In this example, the service is built of only one mapping. The original mapping consists of 1 source, several transformations and 1 target. In this case, the service consists of the mapping which has both service contract and service logic defined in it . After applying the Service Façade SOA pattern to this mapping, the logic is now embedded in the Mapplet and the mapping is simply invoking an instance of the

Mapplet. Now, the mapping itself does not contain any logic and is just acting as a façade binding the service contract (table definitions) to the service logic (Mapplet).

In real enterprise-class solutions, the mappings may be more complex than the one shown above. In such a case, it may not be possible to embed the entire logic into one single Mapplet. Designer can divide the entire business logic into multiple Mapplets, with each Mapplet preferably containing a unit of work and then integrate them together in the mapping.

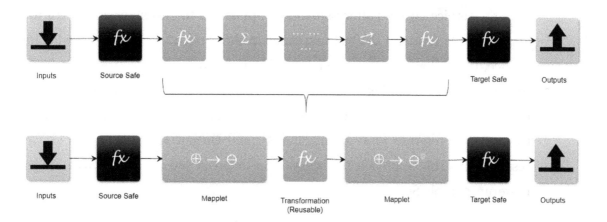

When such integration requires transformations to be placed in between Mapplets, these transformations can be developed as reusable transformations so that the whole set of transformations and Mapplets can be used together in multiple services.

When a service constitutes of multiple mappings, there are different ways of applying the service façade pattern:

    a. Implement service façade pattern to each mapping individually
    b. Implement the service façade pattern to the whole workflow

The difference in these approaches is primarily based on how service logic is built. If each mapping within the workflow is meant to be a task service in itself, accomplishing subset of the activities that the service is intended to deliver, then the service façade approach is applied to each mapping individually. In this case, the workflow will pretty much remain the same before and after applying the pattern.

When a service workflow is built of several mappings for technical reasons (such as performance) and does not intend to serve sub tasks of a service individually, then the service façade pattern should be applied to the whole workflow. In this approach, the first and the last mappings in the service act as interfaces for the service, thus allowing any conversions that need to take place in between. The first and the last mappings together form the façade that abstracts the workflow implementation details from the outside world. The first and the last mappings in this case are referred to as Input Handler and Output Handler for the service respectively. This approach is discussed in detail in the upcoming SOA Design Pattern: Multiple Service Contracts.

Canonical Schema

"Services with different data models for similar data require additional data transformations increasing complexity"

Services operating on similar data should have a standardized data model on which they operate. This reduces the need to apply additional data transformation requirements, thus decreasing the time and effort taken to build additional services. This is not just an SOA problem, but is a general problem seen quite often in IT applications. When several applications are built that operate on similar data but with different data models, the exchange of information between these services becomes complex and additional services are needed just to perform such data transformations. This can be eliminated by properly designing the data models at the beginning of the service development. This increases the design time of the application but eventually reduces the time taken to integrate the application with other applications in the enterprise. While Informatica suite does not provide any out of the box functionality to help such data modelling, B2B Data Transformation product helps integrate such existing services in the enterprise with minimal effort.

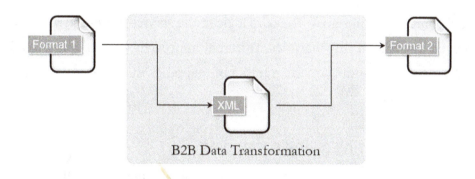

While Informatica B2B Data Transformation® (B2B DT) does not help define and design standardized data models for the services, it helps integrate existing services with different data models easily. B2B DT provides a reusable framework to convert any format into any format. B2B DT also provides several accelerators to speed up the development of such transformations. These accelerators include support for several industry standard data formats such as HL7, NACHA, SWIFT, etc. B2B DT can also transform structured, semi-structured and un-structured data into any of the pre-defined or custom defined formats. B2B DT can be used as a bridge between existing services until they are migrated to a common data model, eliminating the need for the data transformation.

Multiple Service Contracts

> "Service logic must be loosely coupled from the service contracts so that the same service can serve varied requests through multiple services"

A service can be built to expose different contracts or interfaces for the same core logic. This ability of a service is referred to as Multiple Service Contracts. Typically, to achieve this, several service façades are built on top of a service to enable multiple interfaces. The core logic of the service is still the same and is just reused through all these façades. Different approaches are adopted to adapt this SOA pattern depending on the number of mappings that a service is made up of.

Service built using a single mapping

When a service is made up of a single mapping, all of its logic is encapsulated in a Mapplet and Mapplet is then used instead of the transformations in the mapping. A mapping, thus simplified, will only have a source and a target with an invocation to this Mapplet in between. A service built this way will look like this:

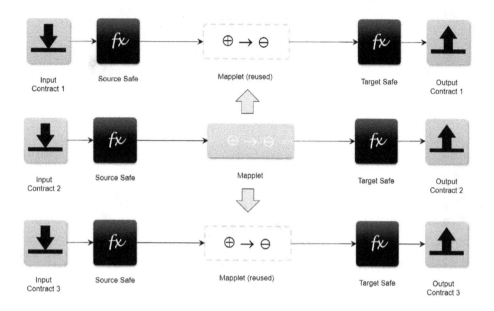

The greatest advantage of this approach is its simplicity. The mapping will have (apart from the Mapplet) one or more sources, anchor (source safe / target safe) transformations and one or more targets. The entire logic is embedded in to the Mapplet. In case transformations that cannot be embedded into a Mapplet are to be used, the logic can be broken up into several Mapplets with these transformations defined as reusable and placed directly in the mapping itself.

Service built using multiple mappings

Applying SOA Design Pattern when multiple mappings are used in the same workflow is a little more complex process. In this approach, all the sessions are encapsulated into a Worklet. Now the Worklet itself is preceded and succeeded by two sessions, each acting as input and output handler.

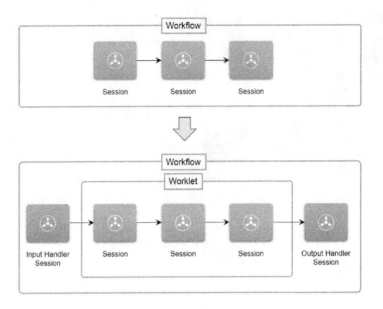

When the service needs to interact with multiple service contracts, the workflow is replicated, with each instance invoking the same Worklet with different input and output handlers.

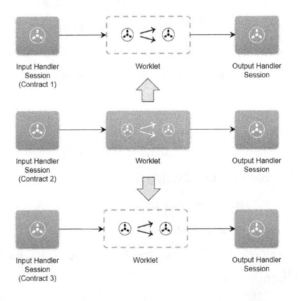

For traditional sources/targets such as databases and files, these input output handlers can be simple mappings. When semi structured and unstructured data needs to be processed, these handlers can be built using sophisticated technology such as B2B Data Transformation. This helps the service to be reused with multiple service contracts regardless of whether the contract is structured, semi structured or unstructured.

Contract Centralization

"Contract centralization avoids consumers from directly approaching the underlying service resources / logic by streamlining the contract"

Typically, by the time a service is built, there are several consumers directly accessing the same resources/logic that the service is built on. These consumers prefer to access the resources directly. However, this causes burden on governance of the resources/logic and gives rise to scalability and reliability issues. Hence all consumers should eventually be migrated to go through the service and its contract. This eliminates consumer-to-implementation.

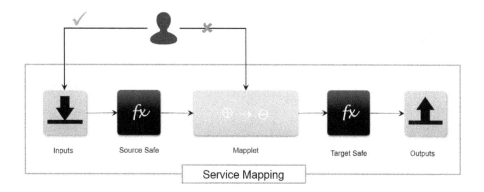

The picture above shows an example of such consumer-to-implementation and how it is avoided with contract centralization. This can be achieved by using the resources/logic in the mappings and removing individual access to the resources. However, this needs to be completed over a span of time with proper plan to migrate the users so that there is no downtime for existing systems while migrating on to the new service

Validation Abstraction

"Abstracting the validations of the contract from the service helps protect the service logic from frequent changes to validations"

Validation rules are necessary to prevent invalid data from being passed into the service logic and hence limit the service exceptions. However, combining the validation rules with the service logic causes negative effects as the service logic is impacted every time the validation rules change. This can be reduced or eliminated by abstracting the validation rules from the service logic.

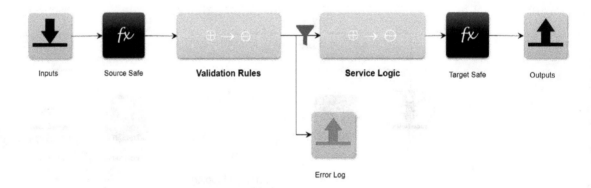

As shown in the picture above, validation rules can be abstracted into a Mapplet and any requests that do not meet specific validation rules are filtered out (or reported as exceptions) before they proceed to the core service logic. This

protects the core service logic from any exceptions. This also abstracts the validation rules from the service logic so that both of them can be developed or improvised independently. When versioning is enabled, the validation rules and core service logic can be developed, versioned and deployed completely independent of each other and still maintain different versions for audit and traceability purposes. The error log helps keep track of any validation errors. In case the data being transferred is sensitive, the error log can be built to skip the data and just log the error code and error message, indicating the validation rule that failed.

Logic Centralization

"Logic centralization helps in reusing service logic and hence avoids building redundant functionality"

Without proper governance in place, functionality that is already built into a service can be redundantly developed in other services over a period of time. Hence, the service logic should be centralized and reused in any future services. When a service is being built, a strict enforcement needs to be in place during the design phase to ensure that the service is appropriately reusing any functionality that is already available in the enterprise. While this is primarily a governance issue, the technology that the services are being built on, should also provide such a framework. Fortunately, both Informatica platform provide this kind of framework. The core service logic can be embedded into one or more Mapplets and the Mapplets are used in the actual service. Hence the entire core logic is divided into one or more Mapplets that can be reused in any number of future mappings.

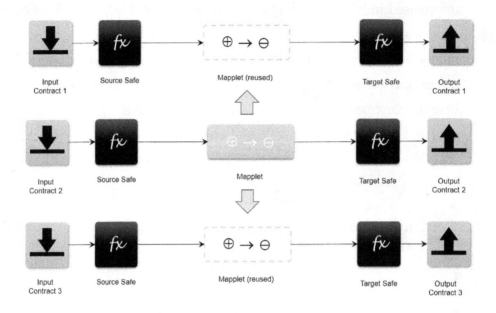

As shown in the picture above, once the core logic is embedded into reusable components such as Mapplets, the logic can be reused in other services as well.

Agnostic Capability

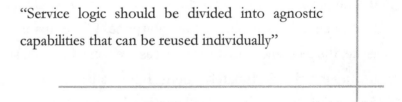

"Service logic should be divided into agnostic capabilities that can be reused individually"

Agnostic services contain service logic that can be reused later. However, at times, service logic is quite complex and is made up of more than one capability.

These capabilities are sometimes needed in other services and are usually rebuilt. This causes redundancy of the core logic that should be avoided. These capabilities need to be identified first before any technical solution is applied.

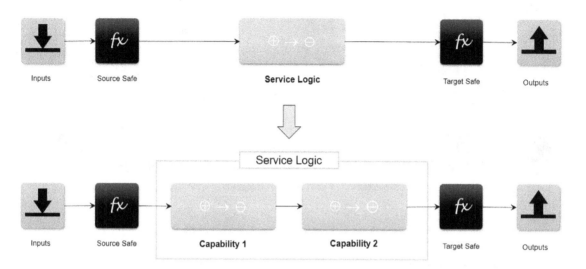

Once identified, these capabilities are then published as Mapplets in Informatica platform. If the entire service logic is already published as a Mapplet, this Mapplet can be broken up in to several simple Mapplets, with each operating on a capability. Each of these capabilities can be reused in other services. Since each capability is an object by itself, they can be used in services by themselves or can also be used in any combination together. The only impact of such a solution is that over time many objects are reused, causing several dependencies between services. For example, if "Capability 1" needs to be updated, it has to be updated for all the services together. If there are a lot of consumers depending on these services, the impact of updating each capability is huge. Hence, proper governance needs to be established around the development and usage of the services.

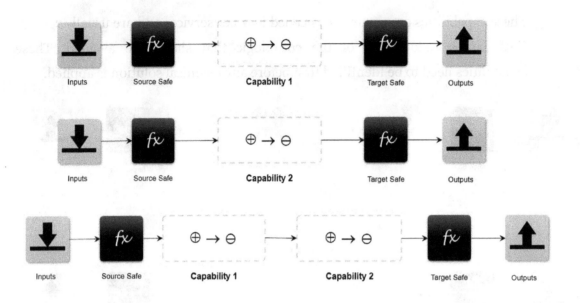

Agnostic Context

> "Agnostic (multi-purpose) logic should be separated from single-purpose logic for proper usage of the services"

When a service is built, it is built with specific functionality in mind. This functionality might include logic, that is built exclusively for this service (one-time) and also the logic that is potentially reusable for other services in future. These two kinds of logic should never be mixed together and should be kept separate. Ideally, these two kinds of logic should be designed and developed independent of each other, though they are used together in a service.

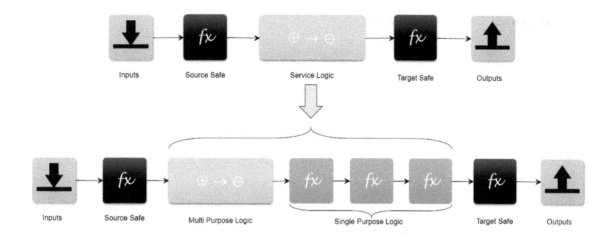

As shown in the picture above, the service logic that is already built as a Mapplet is now split up, so that agnostic logic is now published into the Mapplet and non-agnostic logic is built directly into the mapping. For readability and governance, the non-agnostic logic can also be placed into a Mapplet, but should not be present in the same Mapplet as the agnostic logic. In such a case, a proper naming convention should also be used. For example, a Mapplet containing agnostic logic can be named with a prefix `mplt_r_`, whereas non-reusable Mapplets can simply be prefixed with `mplt_`. This provides a clear distinction between the purposes served by each Mapplet.

Functional Decomposition

"Functional decomposition encourages division of complex business logic into smaller manageable logic modules"

Typically, a service is built to solve a business problem. A large business problem is made up of several small business problems. If a single complex solution is built for the entire business problem, it can only be reused as a whole. This limits the service reusability. If some of the functionality of the service is needed as part of new and evolving services, this logic needs to be redundantly developed as there is no way to reuse parts of the original service. When functional decomposition design pattern is applied, the business problem is broken into several smaller problems and when a service is built to solve the business problem, it is built such that it comprises of different components – each component solving a specific part of the business problem. This increases the reusability of the individual components along with the service itself.

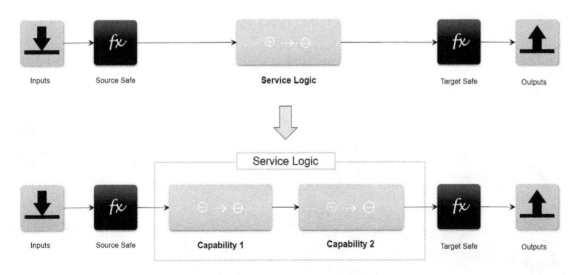

As shown in the picture above, the mapping service is broken into different Mapplets, with each Mapplet publishing one capability. Each of these capabilities (Mapplet) can be versioned and managed independent of each other.

Service Encapsulation

"Functional encapsulation refers to the service's ability to encapsulate its solution logic from its consumers"

When solution logic is built, it is usually confined to the boundaries of its implementation. These boundaries can be expanded and the logic can be published as a service so that it can be reused across the enterprise. If the logic is built within an Informatica Mapplet or mapping or Worklet or a workflow, it can be published as a web service so that it can be invoked by services built using non Informatica technologies seamlessly.

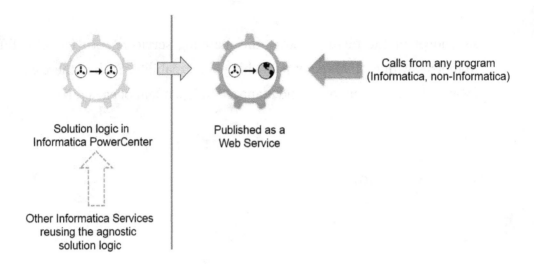

The picture above demonstrates PowerCenter logic published as a web service. The web service encapsulates the solution logic built in PowerCenter so that any program that can make a web service call, can invoke it. For the programs to be able to invoke the web service, they just need to know the contract details without any implementation details. A web service thus built can also be invoked by non-Informatica programs such as Java, .NET etc.

To publish PowerCenter mapping(s) as web services, Logic Centralization design pattern must be applied first. Thus the core logic gets published into the Mapplet(s), while the mapping(s) serve as an interface between the contract and the logic itself. Then the corresponding workflow can be published as a service workflow. For Informatica programs to reuse the agnostic solution logic, they can directly access the Mapplet(s) and/or they can invoke the web service using a Web Service Consumer transformation. If the Mapplets are being reused in other Informatica programs, care must be taken not to have service mappings and regular mappings share the same mapplets. Non-service (regular) mappings must not use these Mapplets to prevent consumer-to-implementation coupling. For regular mappings to reuse the solution logic, they should invoke the web service just like any other non-Informatica program.

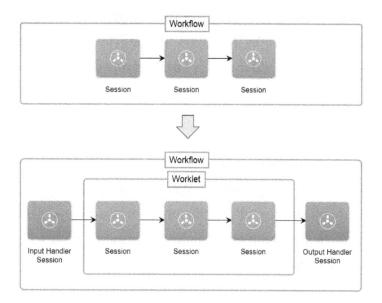

If the solution logic consists of more than one mapping, then the logic centralization must be applied to all the mappings that are part of the workflow and then it should be applied on the workflow itself to push the sessions and tasks into reusable Worklets. These Worklets are then published within a workflow and the workflow is exposed as a service.

Rules Centralization

"Business rules should be centrally governed to avoid multiple implementations of the same solution logic"

Business rules are built to solve specific business problems or part thereof. Each rule represents a set of conditions applied on a chunk of data and an action that needs to be taken when the conditions are met. When the conditions are met, the rule is said to be fired. The action then taken can be a simple transformation of the input data or can be a complex business logic, involving data elements from several datasets. In either case, a business rule defines logic that addresses a part or whole of a business problem.

Solution logic pertaining to business rules should be developed as Reusable transformations or Mapplets or Worklets depending on their complexity. These objects should be stored and maintained in a Shared Folder and shortcuts of these objects shall be used in various service mappings. This centralizes all the rules into a single shared folder.

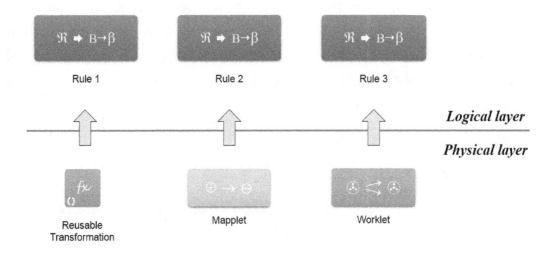

Based on the business problems and the solution logic, one or more services are built based on one or more rules. Rules typically do not have any interfaces and are simply pluggable components for services. When a service is built, it usually has an input contract, one or more rules, (occasionally some non-agnostic, service-specific solution logic) and an output contract.

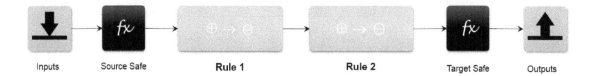

Picture above shows a single-mapping service that is built in PowerCenter. Each Mapplet is a business rule that has come together to form a service logic. This mapping is then used in a workflow that is published as a service.

Inventory Endpoint

"Instead of exposing all services in an inventory, an endpoint service can be built that exposes only pre-determined service capabilities"

Imagine a Service Inventory containing several services. Due to many reasons, including security and governance, exposing all the services within the inventory may not be feasible for all the customers. In such cases, endpoint services can be built to serve these customers. Endpoint service exposes specific services within the inventory to specific customers.

In the picture above, a mapping service is invoking 3 services: Service 1, Service 2 and Service 3.

www.ingramcontent.com/pod-product-compliance
Lightning Source LLC
Chambersburg PA
CBHW080603060326
40689CB00021B/4918